Parenting: A Sacred Path

A Reflection Booklet for Personal or Group Use

by Patience Leiden Robbins

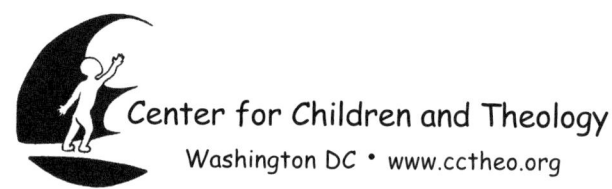
Center for Children and Theology
Washington DC • www.cctheo.org

©2008 Patience Leiden Robbins

ISBN #9780981934518

To my daughter Therese.

ᛞ ᛟ

I rejoice in the gift you are.

Acknowledgements

I would like to thank all the parents who participated in the various groups I led on the topic of spirituality and parenting from 1994- 2000. Thank you for your willingness to explore this theme with such honesty and vulnerability. This book took shape because of you.

I am grateful to the Shalem Institute and to all in the Shalem community: colleagues, friends, associates and participants for your prayer, love, and support throughout the years.

Special thanks to my cousin, friend, editor and publisher, Catherine Maresca, who worked with me for the past year to prepare this material for publishing. It has been an amazing gift to work with you. Thanks for coaching and empowering me and for bringing this book into being.

Thank you to Caroline Bernhardt-Lanier, Monica Maxon, and Kristy Malochee for wholeheartedly supporting me and believing that this booklet was a vital contribution to parents throughout our world.

Thank you to all the following people who offered encouragement, support and feedback: Keith Anderson, Bill Dietrich, Carole Eckerman, Cathy Feil, Dwight Fraser, Joe Grant, Laura Kintz, Ann Kline, Cindy Lapp, Christine Leonard-Osterwalder, Lois Lindbloom, Colleen McCarthy, Mary Joan Park, Marie Quinlan, Lisa Reardon, Mary Roden, June Schulte, Susan Stith, Eda Uca-Dorn, and Judy Walsh-Mellett.

Thank you, Joe and Therese, for encouraging and loving me through this time of writing.

To all the many people who prayed this booklet into existence, thank you.

Table of Contents

Introduction ~~~~~~~~~~~~~~~~~~~~~~~~~~~~~~~~~~~~~~~ 2

One ~~~~~~ 5
   The Starting Place: Know and Honor Yourself as a Parent

Two ~~~~~~ 11
   Invitation to See Anew

Three ~~~~~~ 17
   Service and Self-Giving

Four ~~~~~~ 22
   And a Little Child Shall Lead Them

Five ~~~~~~ 27
   Compassion For Ourselves

Six ~~~~~~ 33
   Entrusting Our Children to God: Letting Go

Appendix ~~~~~~~~~~~~~~~~~~~~~~~~~~~~~~~~~~~~~ 39

Bibliography~~~~~~~~~~~~~~~~~~~~~~~~~~~~~~~~~~ 43

Introduction

When my daughter was three, I searched for ways to integrate my spirituality with my experience of parenting. There was little written that was helpful. There were lots of books on parenting skills, information about raising children and teaching children about God, but I was looking for something that addressed what was going on in me. Parenting was much more challenging than any spiritual practice that I had encountered or considered. It was the most selfless, eye-opening, discipline that I had ever experienced. I never could have foreseen this. As one who had been on an intentional spiritual journey for over 15 years, life with a daughter threw me totally out of whack; I seemed to have lost my sense of direction toward God. So I lived with the question: where is God in the midst of all this?

This question of the spirituality of parenting weighed on my heart and mind. After much prayer, I began to invite others to explore this theme with me in small group settings. As interest grew, I led many groups and workshops on the topic, primarily offered through the Shalem Institute for Spiritual Formation in Bethesda, Maryland. This booklet was born out of that prayerful work: courageous parents who shared together honestly and openly in small groups. Through prayer, reflection and silence certain themes emerged that resonated with all of us. How supportive it was to be together and share in a safe environment what was happening in our lives and what we were noticing about our experience. After leading groups on the spirituality of parenting for a few years, my work evolved to lead workshops and retreats around other themes. I carefully and lovingly shelved all my notes on parenting and spirituality, with great affection for all those who had shared so meaningfully and deeply with me in these circles.

A few months ago, I felt the inspiration and nudge to take it off the shelf and share these reflections – this particular way of viewing the path of parenting – with a broader community. And so this booklet came into being. It is not a complete word or the only word but I trust it will be useful to those who may now be pondering this question of where God is in the midst of parenting.

The fundamental assumption that underlies all of this material is: " ...in God, we live and move and have our being." (Acts 17, 28) Our identity is in God; we are here to love God with our whole heart, mind and strength and to love our neighbor as ourselves. Therefore, we need to cultivate ways of being aware of God and nurturing this love in our lives. It requires both intention and attention. Just as we develop skills or tools for our outer work so we need to find ways to nurture this inner life.

The six themes that are developed in this booklet begin with **Know and Honor Yourself as a Parent.** This section addresses self-awareness and self acceptance. The second theme is **Invitation To See Anew.** This section shares the core shift that occurs as we begin to see that all of life is a spiritual practice as we open our hearts to God. **The Heart of Parenting** tells how the many tasks and responsibilities integral to parenting have the potential to expand our heart to love in ways we may never have imagined. **A Little Child Shall Lead Them** tells how young children model and invite us to BE in the moment and appreciate the fullness of life. **Compassion For Ourselves** reflects on the need for forgiveness and gentleness toward ourselves which then can overflow to our children and others. **Entrusting our Children to God** is an invitation throughout our lives to let our children go knowing they are embraced by a loving God.

Each theme is followed by 'seeds' for thought for each day of the week in the form of simple quotes. I have drawn upon my teachers for these, people who have inspired me by their lives and their words. The daily quote is followed by a suggested prayer response and closes with a prayer you can carry in your heart throughout the day. As these seeds of thought are nurtured with prayer and watered with reflection over the next six week period, it is my hope that they will germinate in your mind and take root in your heart and blossom in deeper and wider love for God, yourself, your children and the world. May this journey transform you and may it overflow with great blessing to your family and all the world.

Note:

The booklet is designed for personal or group use. If you feel led to use this booklet with groups, there is a format, guidelines and meditations included at the end. I also envision parents using this on their own and have included some suggestions as to how to do this as well. It is short and compact and could be put in one's pocket or purse on your way to sporting events, music lessons and other activities, for your ongoing prayer and reflection.

One

The Starting Place:
Know and Honor Yourself as a Parent

In the gift of this new day, in the gift of the present moment,
in the gift of time and eternity intertwined
let me be thankful
let me be attentive
let me be open to what has never happened before,
In the gift of this new day, in the gift of the present moment,
in the gift of time and eternity intertwined.

—Philip Newell

It is important to start here – in this moment – and notice what is authentic and true about your parenting experience. As parents, we may try to live in an idealistic way. We think we should be more patient, kind, understanding and wise. We believe that we should be competent in every situation that arises with our children. We think we should know how to respond to all the various demands made on us as parents and be able to adjust to changes and shifts that occur in rapid succession. We may not even realize that we have these shoulds, ideals and expectations of ourselves that determine how we feel about ourselves and others. This inner script can go on and on until we feel inadequate or incompetent, and become very discouraged. Or we may feel really good about our parenting and wonder if we are fooling ourselves as we listen to the concerns and troubles of other parents.

As we cultivate self-awareness, it is essential to notice what is true and real for us in this moment, for this is the only moment there is. This awareness also requires a willingness to see what we may not like or what might feel scary or threatening, so it asks for some gentle acceptance. Often our pattern is to resist what is happening and think it should be what we have in our mind; we believe that we would be better parents if our children or our circumstances were different. For example, if my infant daughter would sleep through the night, I would be more patient and tolerant. The expectation is that she should sleep through the night so I would feel rested and then be patient. Or if only my child could go to school all day, I could have time to devote to my work and projects. This implies that life will not be okay for me until my child is gone for the day and I have time to myself. Or, if only my parents lived closer, I could have child care and then be able to get a break. I am thinking that I won't get a break because I have no family nearby to help. In all these situations, I am not present to the moment. I am waiting for time to pass and became different so that I can be whatever I think I should be – rested, patient, fulfilled. As we take time to notice what is really going on inside us and in our circumstances, we then have some freedom and openness within us. If we can notice it and then accept it, we leave room for something new to unfold. Perhaps something surprising and unexpected will open up for us when we are present to our reality. And God is in the present as it is – not in the way we would like it to be. Otherwise, we are only thinking about God in the abstract or more likely, totally unaware of God in our experience.

I invite you now to listen to your own inner truth. As you reflect, what may surface is all the "shoulds" and other messages that come from your own or other's expectations. Let them come with no judgment or analysis. Let yourself be open to deeper knowing and what may be below all of those "shoulds" and "if onlys". An exercise with clay is provided to assist this gentle noticing of our experience.

Preliminary Exercise

I invite you to pay attention to your experience by doing a simple exercise with some clay (such as Sculpee). Be as creative and expressive as you can be. You can use crayons, paint, scissors, construction paper and any objects in your house or outside to decorate or enhance this clay.

As you color, paint or otherwise shape your clay, let it describe your parenting at this time – not what you would like it to be, but what your experience is now; for example, empty, filled, grateful, frazzled, frustrated, joyful.....

As you do this exercise, gently respond to these questions:

What are some of your joys in parenting at this time?

What are some of your fears in parenting at this time?

What are some of your comforts in parenting at this time?

What are some of your challenges in parenting at this time?

What is your intention or desire regarding your parenting at this time? What kind of parent do you want to BE?

When you finish this exercise, take this clay and notice again what it describes about you. Take a moment to open all of this to God. Let this clay come to symbolize what is true for you at this moment. Let this clay express your desire to open your parenting to God, – to Love. As Gerald May wrote: "All we have in our hands is our desire, which is at once our prayer, our yes, our hope." (May, 2004, p.195.)

Reflections for the Week

~~~~~~~~~~~~~~~~~~~~~~~~~~~~~~~~~~~ **Monday**

Change only comes about through acceptance. Once you can accept what is and own it, you have the power to choose to stay with the status quo or to make a change for the better.... Acceptance means recognizing that people, situations, and events are what they are. Each moment simply is as it is. Acceptance does not mean that we approve of the moment, only that we recognize that what is happening at a certain moment is in fact happening (Bailey, p. 38).

Personal Response:
Notice and write down any "shoulds" that emerge during the day. Can you imagine letting them go with open hands and heart?

Prayer:
O Beloved, help me to accept this moment as your gift to me now.

~~~~~~~~~~~~~~~~~~~~~~~~~~~~~~~~~~~ **Tuesday**

In intervening years I have often forgotten the grace of gratitude, but on occasion I remember, and when I do I learn anew the mysterious power of giving thanks and how it changes me and how it opens in me humor and playfulness and acceptance of what is. For, in fact, all that we have is given. Life itself is a gift. We are the recipients of time, of the gracious earth, of each other's lives. These are given to us. Acquiring the spirit of gratitude serves to heighten our awareness of God's gift, of the is-ness of things (Wright, 198).

Personal Response:
Take a few moments to notice something or someone for which you are grateful, perhaps the food you have to eat, or your health, or the bird singing outside or the sun shining.

Prayer:
> Holy One, may I have the grace to recognize all the ways I have been gifted today and be grateful.

~~~~~~~~~~~~~~~~~~~~~~~~~~~~~~ **Wednesday**

Intentions remind us of what is important. When we form the intention to do something, and that intention in turn informs our choices and our actions, the chances that we will be sensitive to what is important in our lives increase greatly, and we are more likely to see the big picture. Our intentions serve as blueprints, allowing us to give shape and direction to our efforts, and to assess how we are doing as we work at developing something worthy of ourselves and our lives. So at some point, whenever that is, we have to decide what is really important for us, and then work at constantly keeping that framework in mind as things unfold (Kabat-Zinn, 1997).

Personal Response:
> Write or review your intention for parenting. Put it in a place where you can see it frequently.

Prayer:
> Source of all goodness, may I be open and willing to live into all that you have created me to be for the world.

~~~~~~~~~~~~~~~~~~~~~~~~~~~~~~~~ **Thursday**

Our appointment with life is in the present moment. If we do not have peace and joy right now, when will we have peace and joy- tomorrow, or after tomorrow? What is preventing us from being happy right now? As we follow our breathing, we can say, simply, "Calming, Smiling, Present moment, Wonderful moment" (Hanh, p. 10).

Personal Response:
> Consider this question during the day: what is preventing me from being happy right now?

Prayer:
> **Eternal Love, may I be open to this moment and your love, peace and presence in all of it.**

~~~~~~~~~~~~~~~~~~~~~~~~~~~~~~~~~~~~ **Friday**

The wisdom of the human heart is like water far below the surface, But the intelligent will draw it forth (Proverbs: 20:5).

Personal Response:
> Look at the clay you have fashioned. What wisdom from within does it reflect? See if it needs some revisions and make them.

Prayer:
> **Holy One, may I seek wisdom in the depths of my own heart.**

Two

Invitation to See Anew

Take a few moments in silence to notice yourself right now, how do you feel? What is your joy, your worry, your frustration, your satisfaction? This is your starting place. See if you can acknowledge it, let it be, and accept yourself as you are at this time.

The best way to become holy is not in what you do, but what you allow to be done to you by the circumstances of your life. —Richard Rohr

Awareness of myself and reality was foundational for beginning to see parenting in a new way and how it is utterly interwoven with my spiritual life. Gradually, I began to SEE how parenting could be a spiritual practice.I had to broaden my concept of "holiness." In the past, I equated holiness with certain formal practices: designated prayer times, Scripture study, spiritual reading, spiritual direction, spiritual retreats, and other planned disciplines. Not only was it about engaging in certain practices, but it was about doing them better and increasing them. I based holiness on my efforts and achievement. On the other hand, what I saw in parenting a child was that my circumstances invited me to open my heart and love in ways I never had imagined. I saw that my orderly life was out of control. I turned to God continually. I began to have a deeper sense of what surrender meant; the movement of the heart toward God that is so essential in the spiritual life. Now I saw my parenthood as an invitation to holiness, alongside all the other traditional practices.

This awareness started in the very beginning of my parenting experience. When I was seven months pregnant, I was told I needed to be on bed rest. This meant that I had to lie down twenty-four hours a day, seven days a week for about six weeks. I could be propped up for meals and take a quick shower but primarily was flat on my back. What a shock! I was so used to a full and engaging schedule. I believed I had lots to accomplish! This inability to move out of my bed and home was an incredible experience of being out of control; this was not what I wanted or expected. At this time I was led to the autobiography of Saint Therese of Lisieux. While I lay flat on my back, she became my mentor. She spoke to me of being available for God. She taught me how to receive what was happening, even receive it gratefully. The particular line that emerged and lived in me was: "Jesus does not demand great actions from us, but only surrender and gratitude." I lived and breathed into this wisdom in those weeks.

This was the beginning of what I am continuing to learn in parenthood: opening my heart toward God in all things rather than doing all I believed I needed to do to nurture my relationship with God. Words like consent, yield, allow, receive and surrender had a whole new power to them. This was something new to see and embrace. Soon I lived the experience in childbirth.

In preparation for delivery, I was encouraged to flow with the contractions, to engage and breathe with them. I practiced being attentive and cooperative rather than resisting the sensations and tightening up against them. The experience of childbirth, too, became a reminder that what is essential is the cultivation of an open and cooperative stance before God in all of life.

This emphasis on the heart, rather than on certain practices, is a paradox. I discovered it was not the ascetic practices themselves or the holy things I did to nurture my capacity for God, for love, but my attitude, and my response to life as it was each day. I was invited to accept and embrace each moment as it was given. This often did not feel holy, but more like a loss or a death. I lost my idea of how life should be, I lost the image that I had of myself, and even my image of God. A Scripture comes to mind: unless the grain of wheat falls to the earth and dies, it remains just a grain of wheat. But if it dies, it produces much fruit (John: 12:24). Bed rest wasn't my choice for how things would proceed or even how I thought a kind and caring God would treat me, but I could choose my response. When things do not go the way I want or plan, I still have the freedom to choose my response to them.

This receptivity, the "allowing" which Rohr mentions, is the very soil for God to grow in us. It is to say "yes" to God in the very ordinary and unpredictable circumstances of life, in all the nitty-gritty details. With Mary, the mother of Jesus, and so many holy people who have gone before us, we can say "yes" to what is asked through the events and circumstances of life.

Questions for Reflection

- ♦ In what ways is parenting a call to holiness for you?
- ♦ What helps you to stay centered (or return to your center) in your parenting?
- ♦ How does Rohr's statement: "The best way to become holy is not in what you do but what you allow to be done to you by the circumstances of your lives" resonate with your experience?

Reflections for the Week

~~~~~~~~~~~~~~~~~~~~~~~~~~~~~~~~~~ **Monday**

Each stage of this birthing process parallels my spiritual journey, not a journey of constant spiritual highs, but a journey that embraces a time of desert waiting. My own pilgrimage is one of paradox. Pushing and waiting, resisting and embracing, suffering and rejoicing. ...Too often I have found resisting and pushing more natural than waiting and embracing (Schroeder, p.106).

Personal Response:
Sit with any empty bowl or cup. Let it be a symbol throughout the day of your willingness to receive.

Prayer:
Gracious God, open the eyes of my heart that I might see your loving hand in all that happens today.

~~~~~~~~~~~~~~~~~~~~~~~~~~~~~~~~~~~**Tuesday**

... what is it that would-be saints can learn from other saints? What can we learn from gurus and wisdom figures? Perhaps what we can learn is that they are single-minded. They have discovered and lived the truth of the gospel imperative, "Those who will save their lives will lose them, but those who lose their lives will find them." They have been willing to relinquish everything, all images of themselves and expectations of others, even all dreams of ever becoming great, for the sake of finding themselves in God. They are great simply because they are ever becoming themselves. Yet the greatness of the saints lies not in their doing; their greatness lies in their response to LOVE which ever beckons them and empowers them to love. (Dougherty, 1996)

Personal Response:
Recall a saint or holy person who is special to you. Reflect on their spirit and their loving heart.

Prayer:
O Faithful Presence, in union with _____, may I know the power of your love within and around me.

Wednesday

Love should come first; it should be the beginning of and the reason for everything. Efficiency should be "how" love expresses its "why". But it gets mixed up so easily. When I was a young parent, I wanted to take good care of my children (efficiency) because I cared so much for them (love). This was the way it should be. But soon I became preoccupied with efficiency. What were my kids eating? Were they getting enough sleep? Would we be on time for the car pool? My concerns about efficiency began to eclipse the love they were meant to serve. Getting to the car pool on time became more important than attending to a small fear or a hurt feeling. Too often the report card – the preeminent symbol of childhood efficiency- was more significant than the hope and fears of the little one who brought it home (May, 1991, p. 4).

Personal Response:
Be aware of listening today. Listen to your children with intention and attention. Pray to be fully present and aware.

Prayer:
O Beloved, create in me a heart that is loving and tender and receptive.

Thursday

For where your treasure is, there also will your heart be (Matthew: 6: 21).

Personal Response
Review your intention for parenting and what you have fashioned with your clay. Is there anything to add or change?

Prayer:
O Beloved, may you and your love be the treasure I seek in all of life.

~~~~~~~~~~~~~~~~~~~~~~~~~~~~~~~~~~~ **Friday**

Holiness does not consist in this or that practice but in a disposition of heart which remains always humble and little in God's arms, but trusting to audacity in the Father's goodness (Keating, p.18).

Personal Response:
   Draw or find a picture that expresses this trust in God.

Prayer:
   Heart of Love, may I be as trusting as a child in your arms.

---------- Three ----------

Service and Self-Giving

Take a few moments in silence to notice yourself right now, How do you feel? What is your joy, your worry, your frustration, your satisfaction? This is your starting place. See if you can acknowledge it, own it and accept yourself just as you are at this time.

I will give them a new heart and a new spirit. I will take the heart of stone from their bodies and give them a heart of flesh instead. Then they shall be my people and I will be their God. —Ezekiel 11: 19-20

My infant daughter was totally helpless. Therese depended on me for constant sustenance, care, love and nourishment. Meeting these needs was rigorous and ongoing. She did not consider my agenda, plans, or comfort. What a jolt to all that centered on me – my way, ease and schedule. This tiny person confronted me with all my self-centeredness.

In those early parenting days *Finding God at Home* by Ernest Boyer helped me. He articulated what I sensed: that the service and care that parenting requires is full of potential for spiritual deepening. Boyer talks about all the mundane and routine tasks of parenting as the sacrament of care of others and the sacrament of the routine. Preparing meals, doing dishes, washing laundry, organizing and cleaning could all be acts of love if they were done with intention. The endless chores that sapped my time and energy could be sacraments. "The sacrament of care is expressed not in grand gestures but in small acts which often go unnoticed" (p. 68). Boyer suggests that all we do can be an expression of love, of a soft and willing heart.

But this can be challenging. "It is a difficult life, difficult in the attentiveness and energy it asks. Care is constant…. It is difficult, too, because it asks you to see the extent of your own limitations" (p.68). And these limitations showed up continually as I attempted to be present and attentive to Therese. Being patient with a cranky, overtired or resistant child was a discipline far beyond any I could have invented (or chosen) for myself. Interrupted sleep, cancelled plans, and constant availability stretched everything in me. It was the most demanding fast (from my plans and desires) that I had ever experienced. Respectful communication with my daughter during times of conflict was and is more challenging than any meditation practice I had tried. Using "I" messages and active listening required me to be fully conscious of what I really wanted to express to her rather than just explode with anger.

People often say the greatest gift you can give your children is yourself. I know from experience how difficult that can be for me. Laying down my life stretches me to be my very best self—one that is most genuinely loving and kind, even though at times I may not feel loving or kind. The image of hardened hearts stretched to become vulnerable and tender is a good one for parenting. All the areas of hardness, selfishness and stony resistance are constantly being softened in ways we may have never imagined before having a child. Our hearts expand to have an ever greater capacity for giving and receiving love. As Mother Teresa said: "We do not do great things but little things with great love."

Questions for Reflection

- What are some small and repetitive tasks that you would like to transform into prayer?

- ♦ How has parenting expanded your heart?
- ♦ What are some of your experiences of self-giving?
- ♦ Is there a person who models this open and loving heart for you?

Reflections for the Week

~~~~~~~~~~~~~~~~~~~~~~~~~~~~~~~~~ **Monday**

True asceticism is nurtured by a loving, attentive, contemplative stance toward the persons in our lives, by a willingness to cross over and walk in another's shoes, a desire to be patient and to commit to the long haul (Dreyer, 1991).

Personal Response:
Take a moment today to pray for a soft, tender and loving heart for your children.

Prayer:
O Beloved, may my heart expand and soften with love for my children.

~~~~~~~~~~~~~~~~~~~~~~~~~~~~~~~~~**Tuesday**

I don't always find being in the roles of mother and wife natural. I am in a place where I am dependent on my need for God, just to be faithful to the small mundane tasks, loving in the tiredness, attending to others' needs, getting outside myself (Schroeder, p.57).

Personal Response:
Notice what is difficult for you today and where your heart feels stuck or closed. Can you find an object or picture that expresses what you feel? Can you hold it gently and tenderly?

Prayer:
Creator of all, I am utterly dependent on you. May I allow your love to flow through me.

~~~~~~~~~~~~~~~~~~~~~~~~~~~~~~~ **Wednesday**

When children try your soul, as they will;
When they cause you grief, as they do;
When they rouse your anger, as is their way;
When they reduce you to tears and prayer, as often happens,
Love them.
Don't bother about anything at all
Until you have first made clear to yourself
That your love for the child in question
Is holding firmly, swelling warmly in your heart.
Then, whatever you do will be as nearly right
As it is possible for human judgment to be right (Angelo Patri).

Personal Response:
Make a list of all the positive qualities you see in your children. Express love and gratitude in your heart for them throughout the day.

Prayer:
O loving God, may your love flow within me, through me and around me and out to my children and all the world.

~~~~~~~~~~~~~~~~~~~~~~~~~~~~~~~~ **Thursday**

You must rely on the power of love. This love reminds us to see the best in one another. Furthermore, it states that what we see in others, we strengthen in ourselves. Seeing the best in our children defines both them and us as lovable (Bailey, p. 150).

Personal Response:
Recall a person in your life who has seen the goodness in you and affirmed that. Express gratitude for that person.

Prayer:
Gracious One, thank you for the people who have seen the best in me. May I see the best in my children and all those around me.

~~~~~~~~~~~~~~~~~~~~~~~~~~~~~~~~~~~ **Friday**

God is always present to us. The greatest thing we can do in life is to teach ourselves to be always present to God. The small, routine tasks that fill every day spent in the care of others may seem to be a barrier to this, but they need not. They may in fact be turned into one of the finest of spiritual disciplines, a special sacrament of the routine through which what to others appears the most ordinary and mundane of tasks is revealed to be a sacred act, an act of prayer. Prayer is nothing more or less than this, being present to God. And so this is a spirituality that makes all of life into prayer, a prayer of love, a prayer of help for others, a prayer of courage (Boyer, p. 94).

Personal Response:
Choose one or two tasks of parenting that you would like to view as prayer.

Prayer:
Blessed One, may I be present to you today as I _____ (do the laundry, cook dinner, listen to my children, etc.) .

Four

And a Little Child Shall Lead Them

Take a few moments in silence to notice yourself right now, How do you feel? What is your joy, your worry, your frustration, your satisfaction? This is your starting place. See if you can acknowledge it, let it be and accept yourself just as you are at this time.

People were bringing little children to Jesus in order that he might touch them; and the disciples spoke sternly to them. But when Jesus saw this, he was indignant and said to them, "Let the little children come to me; do not stop them; for it is to such as these that the kingdom of God belongs. Truly I tell you, whoever does not receive the kingdom of God as a little child will never enter it." —Mark 10: 13-15

Consider the qualities that young children possess: wonder, awe, trust, joy, spontaneity, curiosity, openness, delight, enthusiasm, and playfulness. Children can remind us to enjoy being and not just doing, especially in our culture that values and rewards production and achievement . We are often praised for how hard we work, how busy we are and how much money we make. But our children encourage us to play and be curious and notice and enjoy small things.

I know how important it has been for me to have a daily list of what I want to accomplish, and to keep on moving to the next task. Yet I do believe that I am a human be̲ing before a human do̲ing. Being is at the heart of the spiritual life; it is the deep inherent acceptance that I am who I am and I am loved for just being in existence. I have heard it said that we will not grow in the spiritual life until we value being as much as doing. And our children are a living expression of this truth.

Gerald May has written that contemplation is immediate open presence that is directly involved with life as it is (May, 1991, p.23). He notes that babies are pure contemplatives. There is no separation or duality for them. They experience life fully in the moment. What we tend to do, however, is to live in the past or future. Often we review the past and wish we could change it. Or we try to plan our future, but miss the very moment we are in. For example, while spending time with my daughter, my mind wanders elsewhere. I plan my grocery list and I think about when I can take a nap.

May also writes that contemplation happens to everyone when we are open, undefended and immediately present (May, 2004, p.193). This is my challenge – I long to regain some of the contemplative presence of openness and immediacy that I knew as an infant and a young child. This is why practices such as sitting in silence for a period of time each day, being aware of bodily sensations, breathing, or perhaps repeating a sacred word can bring us back to this contemplative presence. These practices, however brief, encourage a return to the here and now and an openness to all that is occurring within and around me.

While these practices often seem impossible while parenting, young children help us do this so naturally and easily. How often they urge and invite us to be receptive and present, fully in the moment at hand. Therese and I used to walk to school together in the mornings. She wanted to stop and look at so many things along the way—she would pick up colorful leaves, notice blooming flowers, or smell and pick honeysuckle. Once when it was raining, she had to walk in every puddle and experience the feel of it, the wonder of the splash, the sound, the delight of the ripple, the joy of getting all wet! She saw lots of invitations to explore while I remained focused on getting there.

We seek balance. We needed to get to school, but what an opportunity for me to enjoy the moment, be curious about what we saw on the way, be playful with my daughter and aware of everything around me. Therese teaches me to listen, notice and relish the simplest things. To sing, dance, laugh, run through puddles, swing through the air, what could be more delightful to God, the creator of all? Through their innocence and simplicity, children can teach us to see things with wonder and appreciate the joy of just being.

Questions for Reflection

- ♦ What childlike qualities would you like to embody (wonder, spontaneity, simplicity, innocence, playfulness, curiosity, trust . . .)
- ♦ What practice or saying could help you play, enjoy, be?
- ♦ Children can help us see with new eyes. What do you see with new eyes because of them?

Reflections for the Week

~~~~~~~~~~~~~~~~~~~~~~~~~~~~~~~~~~ **Monday**

When a child walks down the road, a company of angels goes before him proclaiming, "Make way for the image of the Holy One" (Hasidic saying).

Personal Response:
Pray a prayer of gratitude for all children.

Prayer:
> O Giver of Life, reawaken my sense of appreciation for and delight in children.

~~~~~~~~~~~~~~~~~~~~~~~~~~~~~~~~~~~**Tuesday**

I am the true vine, and my Father is the vine grower. …Remain in me, as I remain in you. Just as a branch cannot bear fruit on its own unless it remains on the vine, so neither can you unless you remain in me (John 15:14).

Personal Response:
> Become aware of your breathing and do it consciously. Let it become a way of remaining in union with God and all of life.

Prayer:
> **O Holy One, in you I live and move and have my being.**

~~~~~~~~~~~~~~~~~~~~~~~~~~~~~~~ **Wednesday**

It is a sobering thought that the finest act of love you can perform is not an act of service but an act of contemplation, of seeing. When you serve people you help, support, comfort, alleviate pain. When you see them in their inner beauty and goodness, you transform and create (DeMello, p. 107).

Personal Response:
> Spend a few minutes with a picture of your children and see their inner beauty and goodness. Begin a list of these qualities.

Prayer:
> O Holy One, may I see you in my children and in everyone I meet today.

~~~~~~~~~~~~~~~~~~~~~~~~~~~~~~~~~~ **Thursday**

If we are attentive to its birthing, children's play can be a gift, drawing forth the lover of life in us. We can't necessarily command it at our beck and call, but it will unfold if we are open to the moment of its magic (Schroeder, P. 21).

Personal Response:
Take some time today to play with your children with no agenda.

Prayer:
O Gracious One, may I appreciate the joy of living and the wonder of being.

~~~~~~~~~~~~~~~~~~~~~~~~~~~~~~~~~~~~ **Friday**

To be childlike is to imitate the characteristics of childhood that are deeply human and of permanent value, the attitudes most of us lose, unfortunately, as we grow up: humility and sincerity, basic trust and freedom from cares, a sense of wonder and joyful playfulness (Nolan, p. 126).

Personal Response:
Spend a few moments with an object in nature like a stone, leaf, twig, shell, etc. and observe, enjoy and appreciate it.

Prayer:
O Giver of Life, I praise you, so wonderfully you have made me; wonderful are your works (Psalm 139:14).

Five

Compassion For Ourselves

Take a few moments in silence to notice what is going on within you right now. How do you feel? What is your joy, your worry, your frustration, your satisfaction, etc.? This is your starting place. See if you can acknowledge it, let it be and accept yourself as you are at this time.

The first response, then, to our brokenness is to face it squarely and befriend it….Yes, we have to find the courage to embrace our own brokenness, to make our most feared enemy into a friend and to claim it as an intimate companion…."The great spiritual battle begins- and never ends- with the reclaiming of our chosenness. Long before any human being saw us, we are seen by God's loving eyes. Long before anyone heard us cry or laugh, we are heard by our God who is all ears for us. Long before any person spoke to us in this world, we are spoken to by the voice of eternal love." —Henri Nouwen

As a parent, one of the things I deal with is feelings of failure and inadequacy. Although I would like to do everything right, I often flounder with how to live out my desire to be a loving parent. I am not sure how to handle situations and then I judge myself as inept; I may feel uncertain and even angry with myself. Parenting feels messy, unpredictable and sometimes too challenging, even though I want to be loving, wise and capable.

I recall an incident with Therese when she was six years old. She scowled at me, yelled at me, went to her room and slammed the door. According to her, I could do nothing right. I felt deeply inadequate and didn't know how to respond. I wanted to stay calm and peaceful but everything in me drove me to yell and scream back at her and tell her she could not treat me this way. I felt caught by my reaction, unsure how to continue or even what to say. All my spiritual practices and any centeredness seemed to go out the window and be far removed from this moment when all my buttons were pushed and I reacted out of rage.

I hear about many such experiences from parents who act in ways that are contrary to what they want to do and are reminiscent of the way they were raised. I remember a dad telling me of his son with special needs and how he would yell and lose his temper over and over again. He felt terrible about this. A mother had an ongoing conflict with her daughter and they hadn't been speaking for a few days. Another father hit his son with a burst of anger and was shocked by how violent he felt. And another parent shared her feelings of wanting to get back at her daughter when she felt hurt by something that was said.

At times like this a practice that helps me to notice what is going on inside is so valuable, again, an opportunity for self-awareness and acceptance. I attempt to be honest about my failings, brokenness and limitations and be compassionate for what I see in myself. Intentional breathing can be such a practice. I breathe in and breathe out, letting my breath bring my attention back to myself and I become aware of what is stirred up within me. It might be my desire for control and to have things the way I want them. Sometimes it is about my desire for affection and approval, wanting my daughter to like me or appreciate me. Sometimes I just feel threatened. Often I do not understand or like the mix of feelings that are rumbling around in me. I usually want to judge myself and tell myself I shouldn't feel those feelings. However, judgment paralyzes me and then I am stuck. If I can be compassionate with myself and gently see what is going on, and even be accepting of it, something opens up inside and I experience freedom. Instead of remaining stuck in old, automatic patterns, we are open to new creative ways of loving and being with our children. As I become aware of what is driving me, I can accept that part of me and be open to God's love and forgiveness. As I am compassionate to myself, this nurtures a compassion for others – my children, spouse, and others in my life. Compassion starts within and then overflows to others.

Questions for Reflection

- ♦ What experiences come to mind when I consider my limitations and inadequacy?
- ♦ Am I holding on to blame or judgment of myself for any parenting failures?
- ♦ Can I allow myself to be open to God's grace and mercy?

Reflections for the Week

~~~~~~~~~~~~~~~~~~~~~~~~~~~~~~~~~ **Monday**

What we need, I think, is to choose an attitude of gentleness, tenderness, a basic kindness towards ourselves. It may be impossible to maintain such an attitude steadily, but in each present moment it is not so difficult. Think of how you feel towards a small child or someone you truly care for. It's easy to feel that sense of tenderness. All it takes is to turn that feeling towards you, easefully, lightly. You know you're good, really, down deep. You can sense tenderness towards the places in you that have been wounded (May, 1994).

Personal Response:
In a moment of guilt, upset, and frustration, take a moment to pray: I am the Beloved of God.

Prayer:

O Beloved, may I be open to receive your abundant and generous compassion.

~~~~~~~~~~~~~~~~~~~~~~~~~~~~~~~~~~~**Tuesday**

Have mercy on me, O Gracious One, according to your steadfast love.
According to your abundant kindness
Forgive me where my thoughts and deeds have hurt others.
Lead me in the paths of justice; guide my steps on paths of peace.
 —(Psalm 51 in *Psalms for Praying*)

Personal Response:
Notice a limitation, a fear, a mistake and bring some gentle attention to it. You may want to notice if there is an image associated with it.

Prayer:
Holy One, guide my feet into the path of peace and healing.

~~~~~~~~~~~~~~~~~~~~~~~~~~~~~~~~ **Wednesday**

In fact, it was sort of cathartic to have to admit that I couldn't do everything, that I really needed God, that I wanted to be a peacemaker, but was incapable of being so. That was the starting point of the conversion – the dual recognition that my own limits were very real and not about to go away and that this recognition was probably in some odd way blessed….

The next step after this recognition was not only acceptance of my own lack of peacefulness but the ability to love it. I began to see clearly what God sees all along – that we are all blessed and broken, gifted and incapable at the same time. But God's wondrous love embraces all of it. Not only did I learn to let God love the unlovable parts of myself – I even began to love them, to try and be tender and patient with my own shortcomings the same way I try to be gentle with the immaturities of my own kids. My heart began to gentle a bit, to be less unforgiving of myself, more open to receiving the mixed blessing and brokenness of those around me (Wright, 182-4).

Personal Response:
Take a moment to notice what inner turmoil gets churned up when things do not go the way you expect or want. Surrender this to God.

Prayer:
May I be willing to see and accept all of me, my giftedness and my brokenness, O God.

Thursday

To see the extent of God's love requires that you really know who it is that God loves-yourself. It means looking into your own greatness and into your own smallness and seeing that it is for both that God cares for you. To discover this love is humbling and liberating. It shows you exactly who you are, then fills you with an extraordinary energy as you find the ability, perhaps for the first time, to love that person. And once discovered, this love opens you to love others in the same way (Boyer, p. 74-5).

Personal Response:
Reflect on your gifts, your goodness. Make a picture or collage that speaks of who you are.

Prayer:
Gentle Healer, may your healing love surround me and draw me deeply into wholeness.

~~~~~~~~~~~~~~~~~~~~~~~~~~~~~~~~~~~ **Friday**

I find it immensely reassuring to know that deep within myself, and within all my sisters and brothers, something is always and irrevocably saying yes to love, wanting to grow into fulfillment. It helps me be more compassionate with myself and others when we fail so miserably at loving one another. It also reminds me that the journey toward greater love is not something to be instilled in people; it is already there to be tended, nurtured, and affirmed. Brother Lawrence, in a parenthetical line in the *Practice of the Presence of God*, said, "People would be very surprised if they knew what their souls said to God sometimes" (May, 1991, p. 54).

Personal Response:
   Take a few moments to draw, write, dance or sing the prayer
    in your heart.

Prayer:
   Merciful One, you are my refuge and my strength,
   I place my trust in you.

Six

Entrusting Our Children to God: Letting Go

Take a few moments in silence to notice yourself right now. How do you feel? What is your joy, your worry, your frustration, your satisfaction? This is your starting place. Acknowledge it, let it be and accept yourself as you are at this time.

Letting go involves radical faith. It means entrusting what you love most to the expansive care and protection of God... We let go not only so that our children can become independent adults guiding their own lives, but also so that God as Father and as Mother may parent them and we all may know ourselves as children of God. —Wendy Wright

One of the ongoing challenges for me has been "letting go" of Therese. It is so tempting to hold on, to cling, to over-protect, to shield her from all possible danger or harm. There are two poles, holding on and letting go, and I am swinging between them. It was such a big stretch to welcome a child into my heart and home; everything changed when she was born. I freely made space for this unique person who is deeply a part of my being. Yet life requires that I let go and let her be all that she has been created to be. This involves radical faith as I entrust her to the care and protection of God.

I know that I would like to save Therese from sickness, disappointment, hurt, and trouble. I imagine that I would even like to determine the outcome of her life. I try to make certain things happen according to my ideas. I attempt to affect or even control what I can. I do try to provide the best education, nutritious food, proper medical care but this does not guarantee that she will be healthy, fulfilled, happy or have a long life. As a parent, I can feel so responsible to make sure things go smoothly and well, as though I can determine how my daughter will turn out. I must constantly strike a delicate balance: I do what I can do and then I surrender the rest. I let go with an open and willing stance and I entrust my child to God.

Times of transition can be particularly vulnerable times, as we may feel the ache of letting go a little more keenly—such as a child's first day of school, the first night away from home on a sleepover, the first time driving a car. Those "firsts" can be real moments of dark and light, of gift and struggle, in which we as parents feel particularly vulnerable-- because it is so mixed.

For example, consider the mother who is concerned for her college-aged son who is driving to New Orleans from Washington, DC, and is responsible for 17 other students because he is driving the van. And yet imagine her joy and delight that he would want to spend his spring break working for Habitat for Humanity.

Or the mother who feels respect and admiration for her 10-year-old daughter who is choosing to become a vegetarian because of her concern for animals, but at the same time this mother feels concerned that her daughter gets the protein she needs to stay healthy.

I recall the story of parents who anguished over a decision with their 17-year-old son who wished to enlist in the Marines. They saw his motivation to serve and to make a difference with his life, but they had beliefs that this was not the way to go about this. They spoke to him as clearly as possible of their values of peace, and their concern that he was too young to make this decision. Although they could not control what he would choose and what would unfold; they could pray and entrust him to God.

In the context of family life, there are many painful or challenging situations that affect us: unemployment, depression, illness, death of a family member or friend, accidents, car problems, severe weather, substance abuse, etc. These things are all part of life; we cannot prevent them or control them; we are vulnerable. This vulnerability is the opening or opportunity for trust. I can freely entrust my children to God, but only if I choose to believe that God loves and will take care of my child more than I! Can we allow for mystery, knowing that life really is out of our hands and that good can come out of all things? We are invited to let go of our need to know, and surrender to God who knows more than we ever could.

Questions for Reflection

- ♦ Can you think of a time when you have entrusted your children to God? How did it feel? If you haven't, what has prevented you?
- ♦ What are some fears you grapple with regarding your children?
- ♦ Who is a person who models trust in God for you?
- ♦ What words or practices are helpful to you in times of distress and/or change?

Reflections for the Week

~~~~~~~~~~~~~~~~~~~~~~~~~~~~~~~~~~ **Monday**

Letting go is an illusory process. It is not as if, in one odd moment, I say, I let go, and that is it. Rather, it is more like a slow process of pulling, taking, grasping, and slipping. Letting go is a process, not a onetime decision. I let go and take back; I let go and grasp, I let go and slip, and eventually, when I don't realize it, I have let go into the One who carries me on Eagle's wings (Schroeder, p. 106).

Personal Response:
Let a prayer phrase arise in your heart that can assist your trust in God throughout the day. For example,

Prayer:
O Companioning Presence, you are my refuge and my strength. I place my trust in you.

~~~~~~~~~~~~~~~~~~~~~~~~~~~~~~~~~**Tuesday**

Trusting God, as Jesus did, does not mean clinging to God; it means letting go of everything so as to surrender ourselves and our lives to God. There is a difference between attachment and surrender. In the end we must become detached from God too. We must let go of God in order to jump into the embrace of a loving Father whom we can trust implicitly. We don't need to hold on tightly, because we will be held – like a child in the arms of its parents (Nolan, p. 135).

Personal Response:
Take some time to ask a friend or family member about a person who models trust in God.

Prayer:
May I taste and see the goodness of God; happy is the one who takes refuge in God.

~~~~~~~~~~~~~~~~~~~~~~~~~~~~~~ **Wednesday**

Then I saw truly that it gives more praise to God and more delight if we pray steadfast in love, trusting his goodness…The best prayer is to rest in the goodness of God knowing that that goodness can reach right down to our lowest depths of need (Julian of Norwich).

Personal Response:
>Take a few moments to reflect on what areas of parenting feel particularly vulnerable for you at this time. Pray to entrust all of this to God.

Prayer:
>**O Compassionate One, you are my light and my salvation, whom shall I fear? (Psalm 27:1)**

~~~~~~~~~~~~~~~~~~~~~~~~~~~~~~~~~~ **Thursday**

Letting go does not consist of ceasing to love, or detaching oneself from the affection one feels, but in loving more. Letting go involves radical faith. It means entrusting what you most love to the expansive care and protection of God. By this I do not mean that if you pray hard enough, God will not keep all the awful things that could happen, from happening to your child. Nor that every evil, even evil perpetrated on the innocent, is somehow "all in God's plan." But that somehow God's presence is available to us even in the mysteries of human suffering and death. Our trust is in a God whose presence accompanies us in every facet of human experience, a God who celebrates, laughs, plays, weeps, wonders, and is seared with pain just as we are. This kind of radical trust in an accompanying God is what allows us to let go (Wright, p. 37).

Personal Response:
>Look for a picture or image that expresses trust in God. Put it in a place where you can be reminded of this posture of the heart.

Prayer:
>**Merciful God, thank you for being my companion in all of life and sharing in my experiences as a parent.**

Friday

O God, you have searched me and you know me.
You know when I sit down and when I rise up.
You discern my innermost thought.
You find me on the journey and guide my steps;
You know my strengths and my weaknesses.
    Psalm 139 (*Psalms for Praying*)

Personal Response:
Look again at the clay you have fashioned. Notice if this is still how you are experiencing parenting. Modify it so it represents what is alive in you now.

Prayer:
O God, you search me and you know me; help me to know myself.

Closing Prayer
O God in you I live and move and have my being. May I continue to allow your life and your love to flow through me. May I continue to entrust myself, my children and all the persons I love to you.
May I know that you accompany me in this journey of life. May I grow in gratitude for the gift of life and the wonder of my being. Let me remember that each moment is a new opportunity and that through your grace, I can begin anew and live out of my deep self in You.

Appendix

Format for Groups – **two hour session**

- ♦ Gathering: have a brief reading – this could be a Scripture or poem or song – 5 minutes *
- ♦ Guided meditation or silence – 10 minutes
- ♦ Check in by each person answering the questions: what am I grateful for/least grateful for today? – 20 minutes
- ♦ Opportunity to read the theme reflections for the week – out loud or in silence – 10 minutes
- ♦ Time in silence to prayerfully reflect on the questions and write responses (art supplies could be available to draw responses) – 25 minutes
- ♦ Sharing in small groups of three or four persons – 30 minutes
- ♦ Sharing in large group – 15 minutes
- ♦ Closing prayer – 5 minutes

Guidelines for Groups

- ♦ Listen in a receptive and accepting way for each other.
- ♦ Hold in reverence and confidence what you hear in the group.
- ♦ Do not try to fix a problem or give advice but listen and be present in a prayerful and supportive way for each person.
- ♦ Speak in the first person as much as possible and do not make generalizations or rules for others.

- Given the limited amount of time for sharing, keep your sharing within the allotted time.
- At the end of each session, take a few moments to examine how one was faithful to these guidelines.

Format for Personal Use

- Take a moment of silence, become aware of your breathing and let your breath bring you into the moment.
- Then take a few minutes to be aware of yourself as suggested in the beginning of each section. What are you noticing about your inner experience?
- Use one of the meditations offered in the appendix if you have time.
- Slowly read a reflection or a quote, noticing what resonates with your experience.
- Spend a few minutes writing or drawing any responses.
- Conclude by praying a prayer from your heart or praying one that is provided.

Resources for Group Prayer and Personal Reflection

- *Psalms for Praying* , edited by Nan Merrill is a lovely translation of the psalms that could be used for this
- *Celtic Treasure: Daily Scriptures and Prayer* by J. Philip Newell
- *Out of the Ordinary* by Joyce Rupp

Meditation I

Recall a time of belonging or closeness with your children, of giving and receiving love...perhaps a time of playing, tickling, cuddling, nursing, let that memory grow in you... see your children in detail, hear the sounds associated with that time, recall what you felt inside.... Breathe in deeply..... let the love and gratitude you experienced with your children fill you once more... take a few minutes in silence to savor this love and joy and gratitude...

Meditation II

Take up a posture that is comfortable and restful and slowly close your eyes. Take a few minutes to watch your breathing—not changing it, but becoming aware of it. In and out, in and out...Take a deep breath and breathe in energy and peace...take another deep breath and breathe in light and energy throughout your being.

Take a deep breath and breathe into your heart. Notice any tightness or hardness? Gently hold your heart—putting your hands there if you want. See if you can breathe kindness and compassion into your heart.

Breathe in loving kindness. Allow your heart to open and unfold, expand and soften.

Continue holding your heart gently and breathing in loving kindness.

Allow your soft heart to expand a little more and recall all whom you love—children, family, friends, wider community. Shower them all with love and compassion. Imagine a beam of love radiating out from your heart to all of them. Let their faces shine back into your heart.

Open your heart wide to embrace the greatest love...receive God's radiant love shining into your heart...allow it to flow into your heart, massaging it with tender care. Listen for these words: you are my beloved child; with you I am well pleased. Take a moment to be with this love and let it soak deep into your being. When you are ready, slowly and gently, open your eyes.

Bibliography

Bailey, Becky A. *Easy to Love, Difficult to Discipline*. New York: William Morrow and Company, Inc., 2000.

Boyer, Jr., Ernest. *Finding God at Home*. New York: Harper and Row Publishers, 1984.

De Mello, Anthony. *The Way to Love*. New York: Double Day, 1992.

Dougherty, Rose Mary. "Unless You Become As Little Children." *Shalem News:* volume xvii, number 2.

Dougherty, Rose Mary. "Becoming Who We Are." *Shalem News*: volume xx, number 1.

Dreyer, Elizabeth Ann. "Asceticism Reconsidered." *Weavings* 1991: volume vi, number 2.

Hanh, Thich Nhat. *Peace is Every Step*. New York: Bantam Books, 1991.

Kabat- Zinn, Jon. *Wherever you Go, There you are*. New York: Hyperion, 1994.

Kabat-Zinn, Myla & Jon. *Everyday Blessings: The Inner Work of Mindful Parenting*. New York: Hyperion Press, 1997.

Keating, Thomas. *St. Therese of Lisieux*. New York: Lantern Books, 2001.

Lindbergh, Anne Morrow. *Gift From the Sea. New York: Pantheon, 1955*.

May, Gerald G. *The Dark Night of the Soul*. New York: Harper San Francisco, 2004.

May, Gerald G. *The Awakened Heart*. New York: Harper San Francisco, 1991.

May, Gerald G. "Gentleness." *Praying Magazine* November-December 1993: Number 57.

Newell, J. Philip *Sounds of the Eternal: A Celtic Psalter*. Michigan: Wm. B. Eerdmans Publishing Company, 2002.

Nolan, Albert. *Jesus Today: A Spirituality of Radical Freedom*. New York: Orbis Books, 2006.

Norwich, Julian. *Daily Readings With Julian of Norwich (Volume1)*. Illinois: Templegate Publishers, 1980.

Nouwen, Henri J.M. *Life of the Beloved*. New York: Crossroad Publishing, 1992.

Rohr, Richard. "The Spirituality of Subtraction" *St. Anthony Messenger Press*, 1989.

Schroeder, Celeste Snowber. *In the Womb of God*. Missouri: Triumph Books, 1995.

Wright, Wendy. *Sacred Dwelling*. New York: Crossroad Publishing, 1989.

Author

Patience has an M.A. in Religious Studies from LaSalle University, completed the Spiritual Guidance Program at Shalem Institute in 1988, and has been a spiritual director for over 20 years. She has worked in parish ministry, campus ministry, and retreat ministry. She has also led many programs at Shalem Institute including directing the Personal Spiritual Deepening Program for five years. She also has been active in peace and social justice activities since a teenager and is deeply committed to world peace. Some of her mentors are Gandhi, Martin Luther King, Jr., Dorothy Day and St. Therese of Lisieux.

She and her husband and daughter live in Mt. Rainier, MD.